King Nonn the Wiser

Colin McNaughton
Illustrated by Greg Rogers

CELEBRATION PRESS
Pearson Learning Group

Many years ago, in a land north of Nonse and just to the right of Rong, lived a king called Nonn the Wiser. He was a peaceful fellow who liked nothing better than to be left alone with his books.

But his people grew restless, and one day the prime minister decided that he must speak to the king.

With his talking raven perched on his shoulder, the prime minister climbed the winding staircase to King Nonn's study.

"Your Majesty," said the prime minister, "something must be done. Your people are angry. They don't like the way you sit up here reading all day. They want a king who can fight dragons and slay giants, like King Blagard of Rong. You must go on an adventure and show them you are a king they can be proud of."

"Oh dear," said the King. "I'm far too short-sighted to slay dragons, and I wouldn't even know where to start looking for a giant. Oh bother, Prime Minister, what's a king to do?"

"Your father, King Nonn the Less, left an old map that will tell you where to go," said the prime minister. "You will find all you need in the armory. But you must hurry, Your Majesty—your subjects are impatient."

King Nonn put down his book with a sigh. He never liked going to the armory. It was full of weapons King Nonn the Less had used, and the dust made him sneeze.

But he unlocked the door and poked about until, at the bottom of a trunk, he found the map.

"This must be the one," said King Nonn to himself. "Giants, dragons, bats, even damsels in distress. I'm bound to have an adventure if I follow this. Now, what else do I need?"

Feeling more cheerful, King Nonn picked up a sword and a lance and went to saddle his horse Palfrey.

While King Nonn was preparing himself for the journey, the prime minister was up on the balcony with his raven.

"Fly away, Raven," said the prime minister. "Follow the King and keep an eye on him. If he gets into trouble, fly back and tell me so I can send help. We don't want His Majesty hurt."

King Nonn's subjects lined the castle walls and cheered as the King rode out on his horse.

He turned to wave farewell.

"I expect that's the last time I'll ever see my beautiful castle," he said gloomily to Palfrey.

9

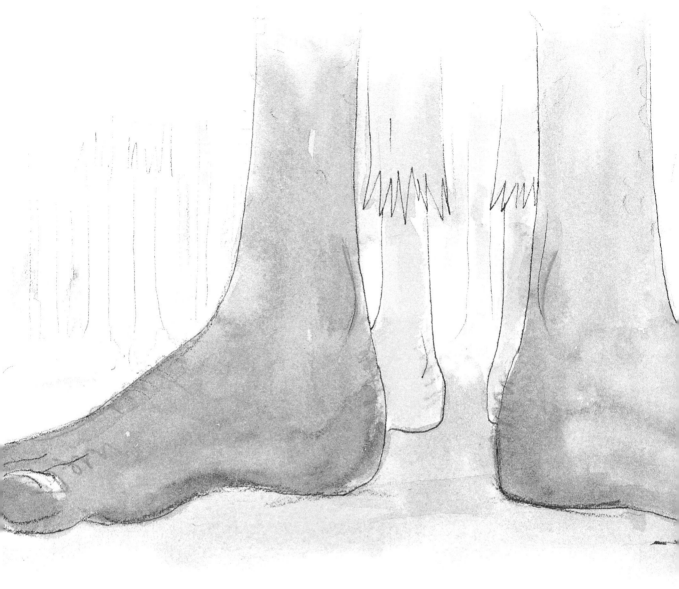

And so King Nonn set forth on his great adventure. He rode till he came in sight of the Land of Giants. And as he rode, he talked to his horse Palfrey.

This is what he said.

"Well, Palfrey, old friend, this must be the Land of Giants. Can't see any, though. I'll try shouting. Come out and fight, you cowardly oafs! Come out and fight! Oh, I do feel like a fool, stumbling about shouting at giants. Ah well, let's press on."

So King Nonn headed south toward the Enchanted Forest, but unfortunately he fell asleep on the way.

When he woke up, he said to his horse Palfrey: "Heavens, I must have dozed off. Now where's this Enchanted Forest? We must have missed it. No wonder, Palfrey—your eyesight's even worse than mine. Come along, we'd better carry on."

King Nonn rode on and said: "According to the map, there should be a dragon here. I'd better leave you at the bottom of this hill, Palfrey, and climb up to the top for a better view. Goodness, it seems to be shaking. I can smell smoke. It must be a volcano! Wait there, Palfrey, I'll be down in a minute."

King Nonn rode on until it was quite dark. As he rode, he talked to his horse Palfrey.

"There's a full moon tonight, but I don't see any bats."

King Nonn rode on, and soon it was dawn. He said to his horse Palfrey: "I just don't understand it. If this map is right, I should be rescuing damsels in distress by now, but I think we're in the Enchanted Forest. Look at all those trees! And I can hear such horrible screams and wailing noises."

"I must do *something* brave before we go home, or I'll be out of a job. But wait a minute, this tree has a door in it. And there's a key. Perhaps I'd better open it."

As King Nonn turned the key, the door flew open—and out rushed a mysterious white figure.

"Help! Help!" shrieked King Nonn.

Palfrey reared up in fright, and galloped away as fast as his legs would carry him.

"Keep going, Palfrey!" cried King Nonn. "Oh dear, I seem to have knocked a knight off his horse. Sorry, can't stop!"

Palfrey galloped and galloped, and King Nonn, hanging on for dear life, panted: "Heavens, there are soldiers everywhere. I've knocked some of them over with my lance. Oops, there goes another knight, falling off his horse! What a disaster this adventure has turned out to be!"

A castle loomed up ahead of them, and King Nonn shouted to his horse Palfrey: "Palfrey, we're home! But whatever's going on? Who are all these people? There are soldiers running in all directions!"

Palfrey pounded over the drawbridge and into the castle.

The prime minister was there to greet King Nonn and took him out on the balcony to wave to his subjects.

"What a triumph, Your Majesty!" he cried. "What courage! Single-handedly you threw King Blagard of Rong from his horse, and single-handedly you dispersed his army, just as they were about to attack!"

"B–b–but," stammered King Nonn.

"Now, don't be modest, the raven has told us everything," the prime minister went on. "How you braved a giant and a dragon, fended off a flock of bats, rode right through the Enchanted Forest, rescued a damsel in distress, and even won a joust with the terrible Black Knight. Now we have a king to be proud of!"

That night, back in his study, King Nonn told the prime minister and the raven what he thought had happened, and they told him what they thought had happened.

They decided to keep the true story a secret. That way, everyone would be happy.

The tales of King Nonn's exploits were told over and over again, each time becoming more heroic and wonderful.

He lived to a great age and wrote many books on the art of fighting giants and dragons. And he and Palfrey never had to go on another adventure again.